ADRIANA LUNA CARLOS

Editor-In-Chief, Designer
and Co-Founder

HANNA OLIVAS

Managing Editor
& Co-Founder

NICOLE CURTIS

Director of the SRS
Magazine Division

BECOMING AN UNSTOPPABLE

WOMAN

MAGAZINE

**ADVERTISING
OPPORTUNITIES**

Info@SheRisesStudios.com

BAUW MAGAZINE *AUGUST 2024*

CONTACT US

SheRisesStudios@gmail.com
www.SheRisesStudios.com

www.SheRisesStudios.com

FENIX TV

PREMIER GIFTING
LOUNGE IS HEADED TO

EMMYS WEEK

September 9th - 16th, 2024

www.FENIXTV.app
www.facebook.com/fenixtvapp

www.Instagram.com/fenixtv_app/
www.Linkedin.com/company/fenixtvapp

www.sherisesstudios.com
www.facebook.com/sherisesstudios

www.instagram.com/sherisesstudios_llc
www.linkedin.com/company/she-rises-studios/mycompany

TRANSFORMING VIRTUAL ASSISTANCE THROUGH MULTIDISCIPLINARY EXPERTISE

Christine Davis exemplifies success and innovation in the rapidly changing world of virtual assistance. With a rich educational background spanning nursing, biology, and business administration, she exemplifies how diverse disciplines can converge to create a formidable professional skill set. As a Virtual Specialist, Christine leverages her multifaceted knowledge to deliver exceptional services tailored to a variety of clients, particularly within the healthcare industry.

Bridging Healthcare and Business in Virtual Assistance

Christine's foundation in nursing and biology provides her with a profound understanding of human physiology and health. This expertise is invaluable when addressing health-related topics or assisting clients within the healthcare sector. Her scientific acumen enables her to comprehend the nuanced needs and challenges faced by healthcare professionals, allowing her to offer solutions that are both scientifically sound and practically feasible.

Simultaneously, Christine's education in business administration equips her with essential skills in project management, strategic decision-making, and client relationship management. This combination of scientific knowledge and business acumen empowers her to see the bigger picture and align her efforts with the overarching goals of her clients. By integrating these disciplines, Christine delivers a unique blend of services that cater to a broad spectrum of stakeholders, from healthcare practitioners to corporate executives.

Creative Pursuits Enhancing Professional Excellence

Christine's creativity, evident in her self-published books "Color with the Word: 60 Days of Peace and Color" and "I AM," significantly influences her approach as a Virtual Specialist. These works reflect a blend of creativity and mindfulness, which Christine seamlessly integrates into her professional life. Her creative endeavors foster innovative problem-solving skills, while her mindfulness practice enhances her focus and productivity. This synergy of creativity and mindfulness ensures that Christine remains present and efficient, consistently delivering high-quality outcomes for her clients.

ABOUT HER:

Christine, a Virtual Specialist with a rich 18-year career and a mother to four children, calls Jackson, MS her home. She is academically accomplished, holding an Associate Degree in Nursing from Hinds Community College in Raymond, MS a BS in Biology from Jackson State University, and a master's degree in business administration with a specialization in Social Media from Southern New Hampshire University (SNHU).

*She has self-published two books, **"Color with the Word: 60 Days of Peace and Color"** and "I AM", a journal. Her professional success has led to her being featured in Woman to Woman With Joanne the Magazine, and Optimal Living Magazine's article, **"The Emergence of the Virtual Assistant"**.*

*She has also been a guest on Author Andrew Snorton where she spoke about her first published coloring book, Blog talk's Women in Business Radio, where she discussed the **"Characteristics of a Successful Woman Entrepreneur"**, and on the Shekinah Women of Beauty television show, sharing her entrepreneurial journey. Christine is an active member of Jackson Woman for Good, The National Society of Leadership and Success, and the Worldwide Women's Association. She is set to be published in Marquis Who's Who 2024. Her career stands as a testament to her dedication, expertise, and the significant contributions she has made in her field.*

CONNECT WITH HER

www.facebook.com/AnointedAssistant/

www.linkedin.com/in/anointedassistant/

PHOTO CREDIT
MITCH C. DAVIS

Navigating the Future of Virtual Assistance

Christine's insight into the future of the virtual assistance landscape is informed by her extensive experience and her features in prominent publications like Woman to Woman With Joanne and Optimal Living Magazine. She anticipates significant shifts driven by advancements in technology, particularly automation and AI integration. To thrive in this evolving environment, Christine advises aspiring virtual assistants to hone their communication and project management skills while staying abreast of the latest digital tools.

Connecting with Diverse Audiences

Christine's appearances on platforms such as Author Andrew Snorton, Blog Talk's Women in Business Radio, and Shekinah Women of Beauty television show have honed her ability to connect with diverse audiences. These experiences underscore the importance of clear, effective communication and the need to tailor messages to resonate with different demographic groups. This skill is particularly crucial in the virtual space, where interaction with people from various cultural and professional backgrounds is common.

Achieving Work-Life Balance

Balancing a thriving career with motherhood is no small feat, yet Christine manages to excel in both arenas. She attributes her success to meticulous task prioritization, effective delegation, and the importance of setting aside personal time. Christine advises other working mothers to practice self-compassion, seek help when needed, and recognize the necessity of taking breaks. Her approach not only fosters personal well-being but also enhances professional performance.

Achieving Work-Life Balance

Balancing a thriving career with motherhood is no small feat, yet Christine manages to excel in both arenas. She attributes her success to meticulous task prioritization, effective delegation, and the importance of setting aside personal time. Christine advises other working mothers to practice self-compassion, seek help when needed, and recognize the necessity of taking breaks. Her approach not only fosters personal well-being but also enhances professional performance.

Commitment to Community and Leadership

Christine's involvement in organizations such as Jackson Woman for Good, The National Society of Leadership and Success, and the Worldwide Women's Association reflects her dedication to community and leadership. These affiliations offer valuable opportunities for networking, learning, and professional development. The sense of community and shared purpose derived from these organizations has significantly enriched Christine's professional journey, providing her with broader perspectives and deeper insights.

Commitment to Community and Leadership

Christine's involvement in organizations such as Jackson Woman for Good, The National Society of Leadership and Success, and the Worldwide Women's Association reflects her dedication to community and leadership. These affiliations offer valuable opportunities for networking, learning, and professional development. The sense of community and shared purpose derived from these organizations has significantly enriched Christine's professional journey, providing her with broader perspectives and deeper insights.

Leveraging Social Media for Professional Growth

As an expert in social media, Christine utilizes these platforms to enhance her virtual assistance services. Social media allows for swift communication, showcases her work, and facilitates networking. Christine predicts that social media management will become increasingly integral to virtual assistance, further underscoring the importance of these platforms in the digital age.

Recognition and Future Aspirations

Christine's upcoming feature in Marquis Who's Who 2024 is a testament to her dedication and accomplishments. Key milestones in her career include successful project management, positive client feedback, and the growth of her Virtual Specialist business. Looking forward, Christine aims to expand her business and mentor emerging virtual assistants. She is committed to making a lasting impact by delivering top-notch services and contributing to the advancement of the virtual assistance industry.

Empowering Women Entrepreneurs

Christine believes that resilience, adaptability, and a growth mindset are crucial traits for successful women entrepreneurs. Cultivating these traits involves embracing challenges, remaining open to continuous learning, and viewing failures as opportunities for growth. Christine's own entrepreneurial journey exemplifies these qualities, serving as an inspiration for other women aspiring to succeed in the business world.

Christine Davis's multifaceted expertise, creative pursuits, and commitment to excellence position her as a leader in the virtual assistance industry. Her diverse educational background, innovative approach, and dedication to professional growth and community service continue to drive her success and influence in this dynamic field.

From Corporate Turmoil to Empowered Coach

A Journey of Resilience and Reinvention

Straight out of university, I embarked on a career in the corporate world, driven by a burning desire to make a meaningful impact in the field of Health, Safety, and Environment. Little did I know that this journey would span 28 years, marked by numerous trials and triumphs that would shape me into the person I am today.

As a woman navigating the then, male-dominated landscape of my industry, I faced my fair share of challenges from the outset. Yet, armed with determination and a relentless pursuit of excellence, I forged ahead, determined to carve out my place in the corporate hierarchy. Despite my introverted nature, I understood the importance of stepping out of my comfort zone, seizing every opportunity to gain exposure and refine my skills. However, along the path to success, I encountered moments of profound self-doubt and self-criticism. There were times when I questioned my abilities and even sabotaged my own progress. Without the guidance of mentors to illuminate the way forward, I relied on sheer grit and resilience to navigate the treacherous waters of corporate life.

Through the ups and downs, I gleaned invaluable lessons about the power of embracing change and the necessity of staying true to oneself. Each setback became an opportunity for growth, each obstacle a stepping stone towards personal and professional development. But perhaps the greatest test of my resilience came when I received the unexpected news of my redundancy and subsequent retrenchment from my job. It was a devastating blow – one that shook me to the core and forced me to confront the harsh realities of corporate loyalty. I found myself at a crossroads, unsure of what the future held.

In the depths of despair, I realized that I had a choice – to succumb to the weight of disappointment or to rise above adversity and forge a new path forward. Drawing upon my faith and inner strength, I made the courageous decision to chart a course of my own making, one that would lead me toward a life of purpose and fulfillment.

For years, a buried desire for coaching had lingered within me, whispering of untapped potential and unfulfilled dreams. With newfound determination, I seized the opportunity to pursue this passion wholeheartedly, enrolling in courses and seeking guidance from seasoned professionals who shared my vision.

The journey was not easy – it required sacrifice, dedication, and an unwavering belief in myself. Yet, with each passing day, I felt myself growing stronger, more confident, and more aligned with my true purpose. Through the support of my newfound community of coaches and mentors, I honed my skills, defined my niche, and crafted a magnetic message that resonated with others.

ALICIA FUENTES
www.facebook.com/profile.php?id=100010655296215

Today, I am living proof that resilience knows no bounds and that reinvention is always within reach. I have traded the confines of the corporate world for a life of autonomy and fulfillment, surrounded by like-minded individuals who inspire me to reach greater heights.

To anyone struggling with unfulfillment or uncertainty, I offer this advice: Take the time to embark on a journey of self-discovery, reevaluate your intentions and goals, and eliminate limiting beliefs that hold you back. Trust in the power of the Universe and never underestimate your own potential to create the life of your dreams.

My story serves as a testament to the transformative power of resilience, reinvention, and unwavering faith in oneself. As I continue on this journey of growth and discovery, I am reminded that the greatest adventures often begin where comfort ends – in the vast unknown of possibility and potential.

JOIN OUR FACEBOOK GROUPS: www.facebook.com/groups/1083015782802570 | www.facebook.com/groups/462810712907548

OZZIN JUN

A Trailblazing Force in the Coaching Industry

Ozzin Jun known as "The Wealth Queen," is an Award-Winning Business Mentor for Coaches & Service-Based Biz Owners. She is the Host of "The Wealth Queen" Podcast for business insights and the Host of the "Inspiration Science" Podcast for mental health talks with new influential entrepreneurs on her show.

Ozzin activates service-based business owners to make consistent $50K-100K+ cash months with a business model that supports their desired lifestyle. Her mission is to make history with bold action-takers, showing them they can have it all: health, thriving relationships, a purpose-driven empire & big bank.

Ozzin has traversed the globe, championing messages of courage, self-love, and resilience. She addresses significant global issues such as religious conflicts, climate change, poverty, and social inequality through her work as a public speaker and coach.

Her profound journey began at fifteen when she worked in Swiss hotels. Hailing from an artistic family, she initially pursued economics but soon realized her heart lay elsewhere. This revelation led her to New York, where she merged her artistic skills with entrepreneurial pursuits.

In 2019, a life-altering tragedy struck when Ozzin was kidnapped and raped. Despite the trauma and missing two months of school, she successfully completed her exams and graduated. This harrowing experience redirected her focus, leading her to study Design Management at university, seamlessly blending her passions for art and business. While studying, she juggled side hustles, learning digital marketing and copywriting, often surviving on just five hours of sleep per night. This relentless hustle crystallized her passion for helping others navigate their careers and businesses, organically transitioning her into a coaching role.

By April 2021, Ozzin fully committed to coaching, despite significant financial risk. Her dedication paid off spectacularly, achieving a six-figure cash month within eight months. Her influence rapidly expanded, earning recognition in Times Square and over 190 publications. By 2023, she was honored as Best Business Mentor at the Global Women Leadership Awards in Dubai, impacting over 15,000 individuals through her coaching. She has collaborated with Hollywood film directors and was invited to Hyundai Motors in Korea, further cementing her authority in the field.

Ozzin's coaching is results-driven, focusing on transformative processes around the "WHO" instead of just the "HOW." Her signature programs offer a unique, engaging experience that guides coaches in designing businesses aligned with their individual goals. She has enabled some clients to make $30,000 in their first month, while also helping established six-figure coaches scale further, ensuring long-term success.

A common challenge I observe is that many entrepreneurs need to catch up with the noise of the entrepreneurial space. They often know what is right for them, but the constant opportunities to compare themselves to others can lead to self-sabotage. Everything changed when I decided to do things my way and trailblaze within my purpose. Being a pioneer requires courage and a clear vision. Trusting yourself in the process will be one of the biggest catalysts. Getting a strategy is easy, but it takes a lot of work behind the scenes to become the person who uses it effectively.

Ozzin's mission extends beyond business success; she aims to empower women globally, activating their potential and equipping them with essential skills and knowledge. She plans to expand her coaching business, aiming to transform millions of lives. Her vision includes building leadership academies worldwide, supporting third-world countries through quality education, and establishing healing resorts. She aspires to contribute as a peace ambassador for the unification of South and North Korea, demonstrating her commitment to global impact.

WALKING THROUGH DARKNESS: EMBRACING FAITH BEYOND HOPE

by Virginia Walters

A large part of what I seek to bring into my work is restoring faith; however, there have been many times when I have been a faithless person; ironically, this faithlessness led me to a place of deep surrender, creating space for something new to emerge.

You see, my friend, Life will betray everybody at some point, but it's not about what happens when Life betrays you. It's about what you do to get beyond that and through it. I'm not talking about bypassing traumas. I'm talking about looking at them squarely and walking through them with courage. Yet sometimes, even this seems impossible, so we cling to hope. However, Hope can keep us idle, turning into stagnancy. It keeps us waiting for the Calvary. It keeps us waiting for inspiration and for something in our circumstances to change. If you find yourself in such a place, don't be afraid to let Hope go, creating a space for faith to take root. You see, Faith is Hopes's twin; he is the one who carries her along the kokoda trail of Life, stepping forward and continuing to walk and live with the knowledge that faith is there and that faith will teach us.

It's a journey taken without vision and clarity, often in darkness or with only the light of the moon. It's taken petrified and terrified with uncertainty and unknowingness. However, it is still taken step-by-step, moment by moment, breath by breath, knowing that faith will ultimately guide us where we need to be, so I ask you today, Where have your walls been stripped? Where has disaster struck? And where have you sat stagnant, blindfolded by the circumstances of Life? and lost Hope? Know that losing Hope is OK; this is a necessary part of embracing faith. What does faith look like? My friend, walk with me, and I will show you that faith surrounds us. It's in the smell of flowers. It's those first chords of new music, the first words spoken through the formation of a new film character. Faith is watching the storm, the lightning strike the Earth, and even though you may find yourself standing in the middle of that, it is that inner knowing that this is where you are and that acknowledging this allows the seed of faith to take root.

You see faith is a journey that pulls us back to heart and into a place of honesty with self, it is the this is all that I have and is all that I am and that this is ok. It is heartfelt, heart-centered, heart-grown, purposeful, and heart-understood. It is a feeling that gives us strength in a way we never felt before. You see, faith lends its hand, directing us with purpose to where we are meant to be and into a knowingness that one day, we wake up, walk out into the room, and realize there is a table laden with fruits from a faith lived in motion.

FROM DESPAIR TO TRIUMPH: DASHANA JEFFERIES' JOURNEY OF BECOMING UNSTOPPABLE

Imagine standing on the edge of despair, teetering between darkness and light. In 2019, Dashana Jefferies found herself on this precipice. A personal crisis nearly ended her life, plunging her into the depths of clinical depression, anxiety, and PTSD. It was a moment of unbearable pain but also the spark of an unyielding determination. From that darkness, Dashana decided to fight back, not just for herself but for others who might find themselves in the same abyss.

Dashana Jefferies is the CEO and founder of A Passport 2 Breathe. Her journey from despair to becoming unstoppable is one of resilience, innovation, and unwavering hope. She transformed her challenges into a mission to create comprehensive support and empowerment for those struggling with mental health issues.

Recognizing the pressing need for accessible mental health support, Dashana created the A Passport 2 Breathe app on Google Play and the Apple Store. This app isn't just a tool; it's a lifeline, offering motivation, meditation, and a shoulder to lean on for those battling depression, anxiety, and the myriad struggles life throws our way. Understanding the unique hurdles faced by individuals with ADD or ADHD, she developed a Chat GPT tool specifically designed to simplify school assignments and streamline time management. It's like having a personal mentor constantly reminding users, "You've got this," amidst the chaos of life.

Dashana's journey has been marked by purpose, progress, and power. After successfully launching her first wellness retreat under A Passport 2 Breathe, the onset of COVID-19 momentarily paused these gatherings but only strengthened her resolve. She looks forward to reigniting these impactful initiatives, providing sanctuaries for mental "well"th and holistic well-being through transformative experiences designed to empower, heal, and rejuvenate the spirit.

Driven by her purpose, Dashana has authored two books: 365 Intentional Breaths and the award-winning 365 Love Letters to the World's Black Kings. These works are more than words on a page; they're a daily embrace, offering love, affirmation, and the strength to face another day, reminding readers of their value and resilience.

In addition to her literary achievements, Dashana is an international speaker, inspiring audiences worldwide with her insights on mental wellness, leadership, and the transformative power of AI. Her sessions are infused with practical strategies for managing stress, promoting mental resilience, and maintaining a healthy work-life balance. She aims to inspire women leaders to harness their inner strength and lead confidently and clearly.

Dashana's academic journey is a testament to her commitment to continuous learning and personal growth. Through accelerated programs, she earned her second Bachelor's degree in just nine weeks and completed her Master's in twelve weeks. She didn't stop there; she became certified in Mental Health First Aid and is currently a doctoral candidate in Educational Leadership. She now also helps others achieve their degrees in less time. This academic journey underscores her commitment to understanding the mind and healing it.

In a world that often demands we hide our struggles, A Passport 2 Breathe is a testament to the power of vulnerability, the courage to seek help, and the beauty of taking life one intentional breath at a time. Dashana's story is more than a bio; it's a heartfelt invitation to join her on this journey of breathing, healing, and thriving, no matter how tough the road ahead may seem.

Let's embrace the strength within, support one another, and become unstoppable women.

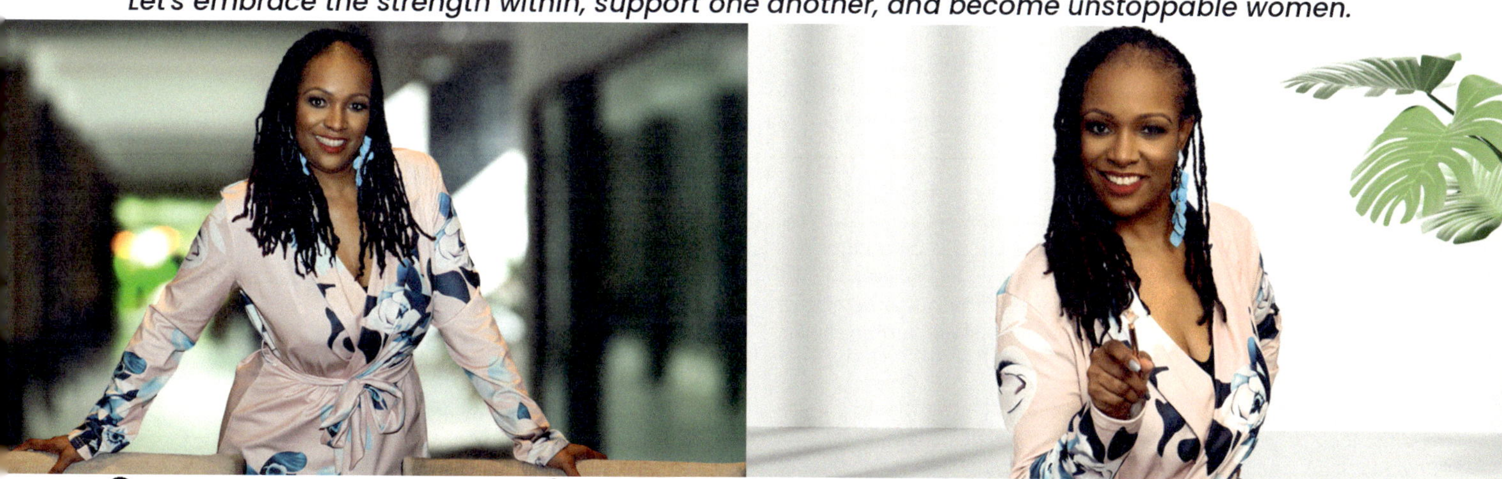

By Hanna Olivas

A LIVE-IT LIST EXPERIENCE AT PEBBLE BEACH:

A MEMORY ETCHED IN MY HEART

Most people consider a trip to Pebble Beach a "bucket list" item, the kind of experience you dream about your whole life. But to me, it's much more than that. It's not something you simply check off; it's something you live fully, savoring every second. That's why I call it a "live-it list" experience. Recently, I had the honor of surprising my husband with a trip to this world-renowned destination. His love for golf is so intense that sometimes I wonder if it competes with his love for me. I couldn't have chosen a better way to celebrate him than by whisking him away to Pebble Beach.

The moment we entered those iconic gates, it felt like stepping into a storybook. The air was charged with a sense of something extraordinary—like we were about to create memories that would last a lifetime. From the warm smiles that greeted us to the shared glances of awe from others who were there living out their own dreams, it was clear this place was special. There's an unspoken bond among everyone there, like you're all part of something beautifully unique.

The grounds were immaculate, with greenery so lush it seemed to go on forever. Every sunrise and sunset was more breathtaking than the last, painting the sky with colors that felt almost unreal. As we strolled along the shore, I was mesmerized by the sight of deer gracefully moving across the sand—a rare and magical scene that I'd never imagined. In that moment, it was like nature itself was performing just for us.

One evening, we settled into a cozy room that felt more like a warm embrace than just a space to dine. The glow of the fireplace cast a gentle light, and the polished floors shimmered as if welcoming us to a place of pure comfort. We shared an exquisite meal, savoring

not just the flavors but the stillness, the togetherness. There was something intimate about being there, wrapped in luxury, yet completely connected to the natural beauty outside. It's a place that allows you to be fully present, cherishing each moment as it unfolds.

During our stay, we witnessed an incredible sight—towering waves crashing against the cliffs with a power that left everyone speechless. Long-time locals mentioned they had never seen such high tides before. Standing side by side, watching the ocean's raw, untamed beauty, **I felt a deep sense of gratitude.** The power and unpredictability of the waves reminded me of life's fleeting nature and how important it is to cherish the ones you love, to hold them close and live fully in each moment.

Our adventure continued along the famous 17-Mile Drive, where the winding roads took us past iconic spots like the Lone Cypress tree, standing proudly against the backdrop of the crashing tides. The beauty of the coastline was nothing short of heavenly. On one side, the vast ocean stretched endlessly, its power and serenity blending in perfect harmony. On the other side, a forest teeming with wildlife wrapped us in a peaceful cocoon, making us feel like we were in the heart of a living, breathing masterpiece. The combination of nature's contrasts—where the powerful ocean meets a tranquil forest—**made me feel like I was part of a dream, a scene so vivid it was hard to believe it was real.**

We spent our days in blissful seclusion, enjoying every moment without the noise and distractions of the outside world. From the five-star wellness spa that recharged our souls to the quirky yet delightful house cuisine that tickled our taste buds, every experience at Pebble Beach was designed to create a deep sense of calm and joy. It was here that we allowed the goodness of life to truly come in, reconnecting as a couple in the most intimate and meaningful way. The serenity surrounding us created the perfect space to simply breathe, to be present, and to feel everything deeply —the ocean breeze on our skin, the scent of pine trees mingling with the salt air, and the gentle sounds of nature harmonizing with our own quiet hearts.

And then, there was the golf. **Watching my husband, with the biggest smile on his face, tee off on those legendary courses was pure joy.** The lush green fairways stretched out before us like a dream, each hole offering breathtaking views of the coastline and rugged cliffs. It was more than just a round of golf; it was like stepping into history, knowing that some of the greatest golfers in the world had stood in the very same spots.

The caddy, extraordinarily professional and knowledgeable, guided him with expertise, enhancing the experience even more. Seeing my husband light up like a kid tasting cake for the first time as he played on these storied grounds made my heart swell. Those moments—his pure, unfiltered happiness—are memories I'll treasure forever.

As we celebrated our anniversary with champagne and chocolate-covered strawberries, it became clear that Pebble Beach wasn't just a destination—**it was an experience that transformed us.** It's a place that allows you to reconnect with the one you love and with yourself. There is no other vacation I could compare to this one, no experience that felt as life-changing and intimate.

I wholeheartedly believe that everyone should visit Pebble Beach at least once in their lifetime. It's more than just a trip; it's a chance to truly live in the moment, to breathe in the beauty, and to immerse yourself in an experience that is as romantic as it is unforgettable. The elegance, the tranquility, and the sheer magic of Pebble Beach will stay with me forever, a cherished memory that feels like a piece of heaven on earth. So, if you ever have the chance, don't hesitate—make it part of your live-it list. Let yourself be swept away by the ocean's song, the forest's embrace, and the simple, beautiful joy of being fully alive

www.facebook.com/HannaJOlivas
www.sherisesstudios.com
www.instagram.com/hannaolivasofficial/
www.youtube.com/@SheRIsesStudios
www.tiktok.com/@sherisesstudios
www.linkedin.com/in/hanna-olivas-93baa617a/

REINVENTING ONESELF LATER IN LIFE:
It Is Never Too Late!

by AnYes Van Rhijn

Reinvention. It's a word that often comes to mind when life takes unexpected turns, and for me, it has become a defining theme. My story is one of perseverance, resilience, and the unwavering belief in the power of continuous self-discovery.

My journey started many decades ago. Like many, I started my career working tirelessly to climb the corporate ladder. When I looked up at 40, I realized I was unfulfilled. I was juggling multiple responsibilities, trying to meet everyone's expectations, and somewhere along the way, I had lost sight of what truly mattered to me. A serendipitous encounter with a coaching training program led me to my true passion. At 48, I started my boutique consultancy, and after a few years of trial and error, I became a successful International Executive Coach.

Leaving a Toxic Relationship

At 57, I realized that to thrive, I needed to prioritize my well-being and surround myself with positivity and love. I made the difficult decision to leave a toxic relationship despite knowing that I would lose everything. It was a turning point that required immense courage and self-belief.

A New Beginning in London

At 58, having lived with one of my sisters for one year, I moved from France to London with just two suitcases, without any income or savings. Starting anew in a vibrant yet unfamiliar city was challenging, especially with a blatant lack of resources. But, this move gave me countless opportunities to rebuild my life and business. I rediscovered my strengths and unlocked passions that I had forgotten existed.

Embracing Change Again at 66

After eight successful years in buzzing London, I felt ready for another change. That unrest led to the opportunity once more to reconsider all my choices in life and business. Fueled by a desire to embrace a slower pace of life, I moved to Croatia in November 2023.

I am now on a mission to shatter patriarchal expectations of what life should look like for women once they can no longer procreate and meet outdated standards of youth and beauty. I champion the idea that midlife should be a period of reinvention and renewed purpose rather than resignation. I help women create emotional and financial freedom infused with purpose, passion, and impact.

The Power of Continuous Reinvention

Reinvention is not a one-time event but a continuous journey. Each challenge and triumph has been a stepping stone to a richer and more fulfilling life. It often starts with small, deliberate steps. Acknowledging the immense value of my life experiences, I realized they could serve as a powerful foundation for new endeavours. I kept asking myself critical questions that guided my journey: "What excites me?" "What impact do I want to make?" "How can I align my skills and passions with opportunities that bring me joy?"

My story is a testament to the power of continuous reinvention. With each life transition, I found new ways to adapt and thrive.

The ability to reinvent oneself isn't age-bound. To every woman in her 50s, 60s or 70s reading this, know that your next chapter is brimming with possibilities. Take the time to uncover your passions, embrace your experiences, and step boldly into the future you envision. Reinvention isn't about discarding your past; it's about weaving it into a vibrant tapestry that reflects who you are and the legacy you want to leave.

It is never too late (nor too early) to step into the driver's seat of your life to reinvent it!

Website: www.thereinventionmentor.biz
Facebook page: www.facebook.com/thereinventionmentor
LinkedIn: www.linkedin.com/in/anyesvanrhijn
Instagram: www.instagram.com/anyes_thereinventionmentor

218-831-1145
Tree Removal
Tree Trimming
& More!
Nate's Property
MAINTENANCE
23

Congratulations Emmy Nominees!

Cheryl Field

Congratulations to all of you who have been nominated or are supporting, celebrating, mentoring or glamming up an Emmy nominee! Each and every one of you have achieved something remarkable, and your hard work has paid off. Recall your early days when you landed a break, received a key introduction, or had a helping hand along the way? We are all where we are today as a result of the 'village" of supporters who helped us along the way. As you step into this new chapter of success, I want to remind you of two essential things: self-care and healthcare advocacy which are neither selfish nor optional for anyone!

Yes! celebrate your achievements, and also take time to rest, recharge your body and your mind. Success can be exhilarating, but it can also be draining. Prioritize self-care by practicing these habits:

- **Getting enough sleep.** Sounds so boring right, while you are sleeping your body is busy at work doing massive amounts of clean up and repair. To start the day fresh you need to give your systems time to do these essential jobs.
- **Nourishing your body with healthy food especially on stressful days.** Eating clean, fresh, light and avoiding processed foods will make you feel energized!
- **Engage in activities that bring you joy**, refresh your energy, and when your get busy define these as non-negotiable, don't ever give up those activities!
- **Practicing mindfulness or meditation.** Remember, you can't pour "anything" from an empty cup. Take care of yourself so you can continue to shine brightly.

Now let's talk about what you advocate for from your position among the "known influencers". Use your platform and your influence to determine what the world "sees". My passion is for seniors, and the care they receive later in life. I am dedicated to growing my platform. After 35 years working in senior care I truly need help gaining the interest, awareness, to the needs of seniors. There are 60 million+ seniors in the US who need advocacy. They face unique challenges related to healthcare, loss of independence, loneliness, and financial security. They deserve well-informed empowered adult children or family members as their advocates. I am on a mission to support them all and I need your help!

- Could you share with anyone you know who is coping with an aging loved one my book, website, or social media posts.
- You can be among the 'village" that gives my voice amplification, makes a key introduction, and lends me a hand in my mission. A short post where you share my story and tag my network makes that introduction.
- Would you share my book Prepared! A Healthcare Guide for Aging Adults" with your networks—both in person and online.
- It is my goal that no senior lacks the awareness they need to navigate the healthcare system, and advocate for living at "home". See the free resources and events offered from my website and share.
- Your voice matters, and your actions can inspire change.

I hope like me that you advocate for causes that matter to you. Remember, success isn't just about the destination; it's about the journey. Cherish every moment, uplift others, and practice self-care and self-love along the way.

Wishing you continued joy at every turn!

With gratitude,
Cheryl Field

Cheryl Field is a Masters Prepared nurse who speaks on behalf of seniors and caregivers all over the country. She is the author of an International best seller Prepared!

A Healthcare Guide for Aging Adults available at Amazon, Barnes and Noble, Walmart and on her web site. Learn more at www.cherylfield.com

Embracing Resilience:
MY JOURNEY FROM ASSAULT TO AUDACITY

My name is Michele Paiva; I am autistic (she/her) and a therapist --and like many readers; I am a survivor of assault, neglect, abuse and loss. Like many readers, I also had the audacity to heal. It's a process and path I am still on.

My journey into the world of financial therapy is deeply intertwined with professional and, my personal experiences.

Before facing significant adversity, my life, like many others, had its share of trials and triumphs. In my early twenties, I was filled with hope and ambition, but a traumatic event would soon alter the course of my life.

I was (sexually) assaulted, left for dead, and underwent emergency surgery to save my life. This harrowing experience shattered me physically, emotionally and financially. I didn't realize then that trauma could have such a profound impact on one's economic well-being.

The Challenge

The trauma I endured left me not only emotionally scarred but financially devastated. The financial strain, coupled with the physical healing, scars that were a reminder and the emotional aftermath, was overwhelming. I was broken in ways I never anticipated, struggling to piece my life back together.

A decade later, my world was further upended when I held my mother, my best friend, as she succumbed to cancer. I had to find the strength to tell her it was okay to let go of her suffering. This moment of profound grief and responsibility was the hardest thing I've ever faced, but it also became a pivotal point in my life.

The Turning Point

The passing of my mother and the profound challenges I faced catalyzed a profound shift in my perspective.

I realized that I didn't want others to endure the silent suffering I experienced or to face financial hardship without understanding the connection between trauma and finances.

This realization was the spark that ignited my transformation. I decided to channel my experiences into something meaningful, leading me to pursue a path in financial therapy.

So much about women is taboo; we are often taught that it isn't ladylike to talk about menstruation, menopause, our assaults or struggles, including financial struggles.

Actions Taken

To address and overcome my challenges, I embarked on a journey of healing and self-discovery. Part of that was being my authentic self; letting my autism be unmasked. Not trying to fit in. It was liberating and I think everyone should let their weird fly as much as possible.

I pursued transpersonal psychology, which combines spiritual and psychological insights, to understand and address the trauma that had impacted my life and finances as well as other women.

I had a career that taught me how women hold so much inside, and suffer in silence. I immersed myself in studying financial literacy and therapy, driven by a desire to help others who faced similar struggles. I wrote three books on financial therapy, sharing my insights and experiences. Additionally, I created the first and only financial therapy app, aiming to provide a unique resource for those seeking to navigate their financial and emotional challenges.

Lessons Learned

My journey taught me that resilience and recovery are not just about overcoming adversity but also about understanding and addressing the underlying issues.

I learned that trauma can profoundly affect financial stability and that healing involves both emotional and practical strategies.

Overcoming these challenges changed me deeply, shaping my approach as a therapist and my commitment to supporting others.

One of the most important lessons is that healing is a spectrum; we may not all be on the autism spectrum, but we are all on a spectrum of healing and overcoming.

Even my physical scars are gone; I was told I would never have children but I did have two. I needed a C-section with my first. My scars were gone because a wonderful OB/GYN when I had that surgical birth, with my daughter, cut the scars away; I didn't know until I woke up that she did this for me.

She had the audacity to heal parts of me that were holding me back, beyond my control- but within hers; and I am forever grateful.

I learned to let go, and use that space as a pivot to create meaningful change, after many tears of course- and sometimes those tears of loss still leak-- but they water and nourish my mission.

Advice for Others

For those facing similar challenges, remember that your journey is unique, and healing takes time. Seek support from professionals who understand the intersection of trauma and financial struggles. Embrace resources and strategies that resonate with you, whether it's therapy, financial education, or self-care practices. Most importantly, be kind to yourself and acknowledge your progress, no matter how small. While I do not wish pain on anyone, if you have it, remember it is an energy and energy can change form. You are more powerful than you can imagine.

Achieving Success

Today, I am proud of the successes I've achieved despite the obstacles I faced. I think my late mother would be proud of me. It is a homage to her. My work as a financial therapist has allowed me to help others understand and overcome their financial and emotional difficulties. The creation of my app and my books are testaments to the power of resilience and the importance of addressing trauma's impact on financial health. My experiences have fueled my passion for helping others, and I continue to thrive by focusing on my mission to support those in need. Don't be shy about your success. You were meant for greatness.

Future Goals

I expect life will get tough and knock me down a few times; but looking ahead, I aspire to expand my reach and impact through continued innovation in financial therapy. I aim to further develop resources that support individuals in navigating their financial and emotional landscapes. My goal is to inspire and empower more people to find their path to emotional healing and financial stability.

To anyone facing their own challenges, I encourage you to reflect on your journey and seek the support you need. Embrace the lessons you learn along the way and remember that your resilience is a powerful force. Take the first step toward overcoming your obstacles and building a future where you can thrive. Your story is unique, and with the right support and mindset, you can turn assaults to your mind or body into an audacious comeback. Feel free to connect with me at TheFinanceTherapist.com

I am an autistic psychotherapist (she/her) who specializes in financial therapy and trauma. I am far-too fond of 80's sitcoms, watercolor painting, tofu and raising monarch butterflies for release in my spare time.

An Immigrant Nightmare Turned into the American Dream

Personal Journey

Background: I'm Arianny Mercedes, an immigrant from the Dominican Republic. My early life was marked by significant challenges, including fleeing gun violence and systemic inequalities in my home country with my family. Despite these hardships, I excelled academically and graduated at the top of my high school class. However, at 18, I faced a significant setback when my scholarship was revoked due to my country of origin, despite being assured of a full ride. This setback was especially disheartening because it felt like my hard work had amounted to nothing.

The Challenge: The revocation of my scholarship was a profound personal and professional challenge. It left me feeling worthless and disillusioned as if my efforts had been in vain. The impact was not just emotional but also financial, as I had to navigate a new path under challenging circumstances. Either I went into over $150K in debt for an undergraduate degree or sucked up my ego and attended community college. I decided my ego was not that strong, so I attended community college.

The Turning Point

Defining Moment: The turning point came when I started working as a hostess at a high-end steakhouse. A regular guest, recognizing my potential, suggested I explore a career in human resources. This unexpected encouragement was the catalyst that sparked a change in my approach and mindset. He shared his business card with me and suggested I follow up.

Actions Taken: Embracing this new direction, I reached out to him. Long story, short, while still attending community college I was able to land a full-time role to help me afford my studies. I transitioned into human resources, which led to a successful career. I leveraged every opportunity to learn and grow, ultimately founding my own career and workplace consulting firm, Revamped.

I relied on mentorship, continuous learning, and my growing network to navigate and overcome the challenges I faced.

Lesson Learned

Key Takeaways: The most important lesson I learned is that setbacks can be redirections rather than dead ends. Overcoming adversity taught me resilience, adaptability, and the value of unexpected opportunities. These experiences have shaped me into a more determined and resourceful professional.

Advice for Others: For those facing similar challenges, my advice is to remain open to unexpected opportunities and seek support from mentors and peers. Embrace setbacks as learning experiences and use them as fuel for your journey forward. Persistence and adaptability are key to overcoming obstacles.

Achieving Success

Current Achievements: Today, I am the founder of Revamped, a workplace consulting firm that has helped over 500 professionals. Additionally, I provide over 100K global followers with free resources, insights, remote job postings, and motivation to help them alongside their career strides.

My book of total client salaries exceeds $10M, and I have accumulated over 7 years of HR experience. I also graduated from the University of Virginia with honors graduating debt-free and have worked with leading organizations like American Express and Accenture. These achievements are a testament to the resilience and determination that emerged from my early challenges.

My words and insights have been tapped by leading publications like US World News, Business Insider, CNN, and NPR. I've spoken on panels at Columbia Business School and conferences sponsored by leading tech companies including Google and Microsoft.

Future Goals: Looking ahead, I plan to continue expanding Revamped, helping more professionals achieve their career goals, and contributing positively to the workplace consulting industry. My vision is to inspire and support others in their professional journeys, making a lasting impact on their lives and careers.

I am also studying for the LSAT and GRE to embark on a path towards a JD/MBA as I aspire to transform my consultancy to offer legal council while mastering the essence of building a sustainable business.

Inspiring Others: Be delusional. Believe in your wildest dreams. I encourage people, especially women from underserved communities to reflect on their own challenges and view them as opportunities for growth. No will always mean no if you let it.

Take the first step towards overcoming obstacles by embracing new opportunities and seeking support. Remember, resilience and a positive mindset can transform setbacks into powerful catalysts for success.

Website: www.ariannymercedes.com

Instagram: (@Ariannymercedess) www.instagram.com/ariannymercedess

Twitter: (@Ariannnyy_) www.x.com/ariannnyy_

LinkedIn: www.linkedin.com/in/arianny

ELIZABETH REECE: GUIDING CLIENTS TO BREAK THROUGH RECOVERY CEILINGS WITH HOLISTIC COACHING

Elizabeth *Reece* is a renowned coach dedicated to helping clients enhance their well-being and break through recovery ceilings. By integrating Positive Psychology, Coaching Psychology, and spiritual principles from the 12-Step program, Elizabeth facilitates profound breakthroughs for her clients. She believes deeply in the inherent strength and capabilities of every individual.

Elizabeth is committed to ensuring her clients never feel alone or confused on their journey. She aims to elevate both her own baseline and that of her clients throughout the coaching process. One of her first steps involves discovering clients' values in action strengths using the VIA Character Strengths survey. This often reveals surprising and unique strengths that clients were unaware of.

She emphasizes the importance of operating within one's primary strengths, which she views as God-given gifts essential for fulfillment. Elizabeth cautions against overemphasizing common lesser strengths, such as self-regulation and judgment, which can lead to burnout. Instead, she encourages leveraging primary strengths to sustainably develop these lesser strengths.

Central to Elizabeth's approach are spiritual principles like Acceptance, Hope, Faith, Courage, Honesty, Patience, Humility, Willingness, Love, Integrity, Self-Discipline, and Service. Living in Step 12 of the 12-Step program is a way of life for her, demonstrating how these principles can profoundly change lives. Positive Psychology also plays a significant role in her coaching, with interventions designed to elevate well-being.

One such intervention is the Best Possible Self exercise, which involves writing about traumatic events or future dream scenarios. This exercise has been shown to produce positive effects lasting up to six weeks.

Elizabeth's holistic approach includes modalities like NLP, CBT, EFT, hypnotic language, and traditional coaching structures. These techniques foster self-leadership, autonomy, and self-reliance, helping clients trust their intuition, make confident decisions, and believe in their worthiness.

Her diverse experiences, from workplace consultancy to becoming a professional coach and chef, have shaped her current philosophy. Elizabeth's core strengths—Honesty, Spirituality, Hope, Love of Learning, and Appreciation of Beauty and Excellence—remain consistent, reflecting her commitment to operating within her strengths. In her consultancy career, she co-created productive workspaces but often questioned if they truly supported individual well-being. She found that superficial enhancements could not address deeper issues like toxic behavior and burnout.

In 2018, Elizabeth left consultancy to retrain during the pandemic. Unexpectedly, she worked in the kitchen of a 2-star Michelin chef, embracing the role and learning the value of a spiritual workplace where she felt she belonged. Now in the South of France, Elizabeth combines her skills to create community through coaching, cooking, and connecting. She works alongside others to provide real, safe spaces, contributing to her happiness and fulfillment. Elizabeth has developed workshops like "Workplace Spirituality Integration for Elevated Wellbeing" and "Strengths, Superpowers & Service."

The former introduces the concept of a Higher Power to struggling team members, fostering belief in a power greater than themselves. The latter addresses the challenge of loneliness for solopreneurs and small business owners, encouraging work-life integration and job crafting to leverage strengths. Her retreats in the South of France offer a serene escape for participants, providing a safe space for sobriety, personal growth, and stepping out of comfort zones. Surrounded by nature, attendees leave feeling calmer and equipped with tools to sustain positive emotions and practices.

As a Masters Level 7 Coach, EMCC Practitioner, and NLP Master Practitioner, Elizabeth employs strategies to help clients navigate significant life transitions. Whether overcoming addiction, leaving toxic workplaces, or escaping abusive relationships, her holistic approach ensures clients emerge stronger, more self-reliant, and confident in their abilities. Through a blend of science, spirituality, and practical coaching techniques, Elizabeth Reece empowers individuals to transform their lives and achieve lasting fulfillment.

Connect With *Elizabeth*

- www.quietwaters.space/
- www.quietwatersretreats.com (COMING SOON)
- www.facebook.com/elizabethreece.coaching/
- www.instagram.com/seeking_quietwaters/
- www.instagram.com/quietwaters_coaching/
- www.linkedin.com/in/elizabeth-reece-msc-appcp-26357a14/

AUTHOR
Spotlights

MEET
Susan
Heartlight
MASTER SPIRITUAL GUIDE
FEATURED ON
DRIVE TO SUCCESS PODCAST

ONE
POWER
FOR
GOOD
ACTIONS TO CREATE
JOY IN YOUR LIFE
SUSAN
HEARTLIGHT
AWARD-WINNING AUTHOR
FOREWORD BY RAYMOND AARON
ONE POWER FOR GOOD
SUSAN HEARTLIGHT
ONE POWER FOR GOOD
SUSAN HEARTLIGHT
ONE POWER FOR GOOD
SUSAN HEARTLIGHT

ONE POWER FOR GOOD
IGNITES YOUR SPIRIT
FOCUS, ALIGN, BELIEVE YOUR TRUTH
HEARTLIGHT360.COM

UNSTOPPABLE WOMAN DARES EXECUTIVES TO LEAD WITH A FIERCE HEART

by Merilee Kern, MBA

Relational leadership and management authority Cheryl L. Mason, J.D. is a force of nature. TEDx speaker, author and CEO, Mason his hell bent on helping C-suite executives, senior leaders, companies, and teams develop the skills and tools to lead with authenticity and empathy. As the fourth Presidentially-appointed, Senate-confirmed—and first woman and military spouse—to serve as the CEO/Chairman of the VA Board of Veterans' Appeals prior to starting her own Catalyst Leadership Management business consultancy, Mason is revered for leading with an impactful morale-boosting, people-centric approach—and teaching other managers how to do the same.

Mason brings a unique perspective on adversity and challenges by viewing them as pivotal moments for learning and growth. Additionally, she addresses and highlights the negative impact of invisible "phantom" leaders on the people and the organization. Her consultancy services help CEOs, senior leaders, companies, and teams develop the skills and tools to lead with authenticity and relate with empathy. Mason's mission is to help other business leaders discover and embrace the power of authenticity—being real, caring, relatable, accessible and engaging with each leader's most valuable asset: the people they lead and impact.

As an author and a TEDx speaker, Mason shares insights and stories about people, obstacles, purpose, impact and mindset along with tactical ways leaders can elevate results. Mason is more than a speaker; she's a dynamic force of nature. Her captivating keynote presentations have graced the TEDx stage and have left a profound mark on corporations and nonprofits alike. With her wealth of knowledge, real-world experience, and infectious enthusiasm for leadership, Mason has inspired countless individuals to reach their full potential and take their leadership skills to new heights. She shares her inspiring journey of overcoming life's challenges, while seamlessly incorporating valuable lessons on leadership, vulnerability, and courage. Her ability to connect with business and corporate audiences leaves a lasting impact, empowering others to face adversity with resilience and determination.

Merilee Kern, MBA is an internationally-regarded brand strategist and analyst who reports on noteworthy industry change makers, movers, shakers and innovators across all B2B and B2C categories. Connect with her at LinkedIn www.LinkedIn.com/in/MerileeKern.

In her book, "Dare to Relate: Leading with a Fierce Heart," which emphasizes the significance of cultivating strong relationships within your workforce, Mason shares her journey and unveils her unconventional, yet highly effective approach to leadership.

The book highlights how investing time, technology and finances into the employee pool can spur long-term savings substantial bottom line results. The book highlights how relational leadership enhances staff well-being and drives success for leaders and their organizations at large. Through relatable personal stories and insights from her network, Mason's book not only encourages and guides aspirationals to find their own inner leader, but also emphasizes the importance of purposefully impacting the world today and tomorrow.

Mason realized an exceptional career at the Department of Veterans Affairs, beginning as a young attorney and climbing the ranks to eventually become the first woman and military spouse—and senate confirmed—Chairman of the Board of Veterans' Appeals. As the CEO leading over 1200 people serving the veteran and stakeholder communities, she implemented technological innovations to benefit both her employees and customers. Through collaboration with her team, she achieved remarkable results, doubling customer outcomes and increasing morale, retention, and trust. Mason not only successfully grew and managed a large budget but also built and led the most diverse team of people in our history.

With over 30 years of dedicated federal service, coupled with her role as a USAF military spouse, Mason held various challenging positions in the legal and administrative domains. Her accomplishments include establishing an educational program for service members and their families in Germany, managing a diverse range of USAFE support programs encompassing contracts, personnel, budget, and IT, and spearheading a large-scale complex legal operation at the Department of Veterans Affairs (VA). Throughout her career, she has earned a well-deserved reputation as an inspiring leader, placing utmost importance on her team, their families, and the successful accomplishment of their mission.

As Chairman of the Board of Veterans' Appeals at the VA, she led a team of 1200 personnel, including veterans law judges, attorneys, and operations and administrative professionals, and executed a budget of $228 million to meet the Board's mission of conducting hearings and deciding appeals on benefits and services for veterans and their families. As a principal, she advised the Secretary of the VA on diverse matters, from wide-ranging veterans' issues to stakeholder concerns. She implemented revolutionary technological innovations, streamlined processes, and created cost-saving solutions. She improved operations by creating consistency in management practices and championed the investment in personnel by securing more than 65 percent in budget increases over 4 years. She is credited with turning the Board from a dysfunctional organization with low morale and trust and lackluster results into a high-functioning organization, delivering results to veterans and increasing trust and morale in her employees through her people-focused leadership style.

Mason served as Interim Principal Deputy Vice Chairman at the Board of Veterans' Appeals where she was responsible for legislation, regulation, and policy, which included building a diverse political alliance to build consensus with VA leadership, stakeholders and Congress to gain passage of the Veterans Appeals Improvement and Modernization Act of 2017.

Additionally, Mason held a variety of positions, including Deputy Vice Chairman and Veterans Law Judge at the Board, attorney with the Federal Labor Relations Authority, and a Department of the Air Force civilian at HQ United States Air Forces in Europe at Ramstein Air Base, Germany. Mason also served as a contract attorney investigator for the Department of Justice Civil Rights Division specializing in the Americans with Disabilities Act; a military services paralegal coordinator for Europe with Central Texas College; and an instructor at Central Texas College, Kapaun Air Station, Germany.

She also served as a PREVENTS Task Force Ambassador, along with Lead Ambassador Second Lady Karen Pence. PREVENTS was the first national public health campaign to address suicide prevention. Mason also worked closely with First Lady Dr. Jill Biden's Joining Forces initiative to address the challenges and issues of military and veteran families.

In recognition of her fierce commitment and actions around military spouse employment and transitioning veterans, Mason received the Hiring Our Heroes 2022 Bonnie Amos Lifetime Achievement Impact Award from the US Chamber of Commerce. Mason was recognized by Disabled American Veterans as the 2021 Outstanding Federal Executive and received the FedHealthIT 2020 Leading for Impact: Women in Leadership Award.

Mason's extraordinary journey stands as a testament to her unwavering dedication and exceptional leadership prowess. Being a catalyst leader involves facing challenges, overcoming obstacles, and genuinely caring for and supporting your employees.

So, You Want to be a Life Coach? is an easy-to-follow workbook for aspiring life coaches and entrepreneurs, providing practical guidance, and personal insights to help you start and manage your life coaching business.

What You'll Learn:

- Evaluating your current journey
- Getting started
- Essential tools

- Business management
- Marketing strategies
- Comprehensive resources for success

"What makes you ready to be a coach is the desire and passion to help others learn about themselves and help them grow into their best version of themselves. Although you may never feel fully ready, you must take the plunge because this is something you have envision, visioned, and created a mission for. It is now your time rise up and do what you been chosen and called to do."

~ C.Coreano

Each chapter includes inspirational quotes, motivation, and self-reflection exercises to help you:

- Define your vision and mission statements
- Develop your branding package

- Enhance your marketing skills
- Build your online and social media presence

This book will inspire you to continue to work on your dreams of becoming a life coach. It provides you with plethora of tools to help you be prepared to take on the challenge of becoming an entrepreneur with the tools necessary to be a successful business owner and an excellent Life Coach.

Empower Global Coaching was founded by Claribel Coreano, and officially opened for business in 2023. To learn more about Empower Global Coaching please visit:

 www.empowerglobalcoaching.com    egc_2325@empowerglobalcoaching.com

From Diagnosis to the Red Carpet:

Hanna Olivas, Chief Branding Officer of She Rises Studios and FENIX TV, Proves Dreams Have No Limits

Hanna Olivas, the powerhouse Chief Branding Officer of She Rises Studios and FENIX TV, is set to make a grand entrance on the red carpet at this year's Emmy Awards, where she will also host the prestigious FENIX TV Premier Gifting Suite for Emmys week. Hanna's journey is a testament to the unyielding spirit of resilience, having turned a terminal diagnosis of rare blood cancer, multiple myeloma, into a mission to inspire women worldwide.

Hanna Olivas's story is one of extraordinary courage and unwavering determination. When diagnosed with multiple myeloma, Hanna chose not to let the terminal illness define her life. Instead, she channeled her will to live into creating She Rises Studios, a groundbreaking platform dedicated to empowering women entrepreneurs, and FENIX TV, an innovative online streaming service.

"Facing a terminal diagnosis made me realize that every moment is precious," said Hanna Olivas. "I wanted to leave a legacy that would inspire women to pursue their dreams, no matter the obstacles."

Hanna's efforts have not gone unnoticed. She has been featured in hundreds of media appearances, including the Today Show, Tamron Hall, People Magazine, and more. Her compelling story and magnetic presence have made her a beacon of hope for countless women striving to overcome their own challenges.

This year, Hanna's journey comes full circle as she walks the red carpet at the Emmys, a symbol of her triumph over adversity. Hosting the FENIX TV Emmys Gifting Suite in Beverly Hills, she brings together Hollywood's elite to celebrate not only the industry's best but also the indomitable human spirit.

Hanna Olivas is a shining example of how dreams can come true regardless of the hurdles life throws at us," said Hanna Olivas, CEO of She Rises Studios. "Her story is an inspiration to all, showing that with passion and perseverance, anything is possible."

Hanna's mission goes beyond business success. Through She Rises Studios and FENIX TV, she aims to create a supportive community for women, providing the resources and encouragement they need to succeed in their entrepreneurial endeavors.

As Hanna graces the Emmy Awards red carpet and hosts the FENIX TV Emmys Gifting Suite, she stands as a living testament to the power of resilience, determination, and the unwavering belief that no diagnosis can define one's destiny.

About She Rises Studios

She Rises Studios is a leading platform dedicated to empowering women entrepreneurs through resources, education, and community support. Founded by Hanna Olivas, the studio aims to inspire and elevate women to achieve their fullest potential.

FENIX TV is an innovative online streaming platform that showcases a diverse array of content, focusing on empowerment, inspiration, and education. It is committed to providing a platform for voices that deserve to be heard and stories that need to be told.

About FENIX TV

Hanna Olivas's journey is a powerful reminder that dreams are achievable, no matter the challenges faced along the way. Her story continues to inspire and uplift women around the world, proving that with grit and determination, anything is possible!

www.facebook.com/HannaJOlivas
www.sherisesstudios.com
www.instagram.com/hannaolivasofficial
www.youtube.com/@SheRIsesStudios
www.tiktok.com/@sherisesstudios
www.linkedin.com/in/hanna-olivas-93baa617a

by Pauline Grouette

Going from Accountability to Abundance with Grace

Do you remember the Tooth Fairy, Santa Claus, the Easter Bunny, Jack Frost, or the Sandman? Childhood figures co-exist to help a child navigate the challenges life presents them with. Magic is believing before seeing, and having faith requires no evidence. To adults these energetic beings may be imaginary though as children, do you remember how real they felt? They all had magic that we believed in so our dreams would come true. I know I did. It has been proven through various studies that from newborn to age seven, this is the most influential time in our life. As a child with limited life experience it was easier to have faith that these 'people' were looking out for us, than the cold reality that exists.

As I grew into adulthood, faith diminished and life unleashed the harsh realities that are in many people's lives. After living through abuse, rape, suicidal ideologies, abandonment, single parenthood, I always knew that I was deserving of more. I simply needed to figure out how to process what was presented to me and over time I kept making it to the other side. Sometimes a curveball would be thrown and I would need to decide whether I wanted to navigate around it or hit it straight on! I am not a baseball guru and I will not pretend to be, but what I do know is that in order to live your life to its fullest, having faith in something needs to be present.

While on a life changing retreat in Peru, I learned more profoundly, that faith is unique for everyone. One could have faith in God, a rock, the Universe, or the most powerful in my opinion is oneself. No one knows you like you. Learning to listen to your intuition (magic or superconscious) made me aware of the actions or events that can emotionally paralyse you or be the catalyst for change.

Photo Credit to Darren Larkman

After my second divorce, and my children were grown, I was given my sign that the energy, or my faith, still existed. I was rear-ended by a semi truck on the highway carrying water so I was hit twice, as the water swished back and forth in the trailer. I barely had a scratch on the outside, the inside was much different. This experience made me realise how I got caught up with the responsibilities of life as I navigated through victim mode, then survival mode and finally decided enough was enough! Those childhood beliefs resurfaced the hope that dreams can come true. My dreams of creating an environment where unconditional love and non-judgement became my reality were alive! I decided to dedicate the rest of my life to sharing that energy with others by creating a sanctuary where others could also start to live again.

Acceptance of my faults, forgiveness of my mistakes, reconnecting with my inner child allowed me to become the leader and Alchemist I am today. I allowed myself to process what needed to be so I could serve my clients how I needed. I continued to forgive all those who hurt me, my ancestors were brought more peace and the chains that once held me down, were now broken. The ripples of my actions have taken effect.

The magical energy, or faith in oneself, that has been in my life continues to bless me as an author, CBT practitioner, Vision Board Facilitator and Fulfillment Mentor! As CEO of Guided Journey Coaching, I take pride in guiding my clients from accountability to abundance. Allow your renaissance to unfold!

www.guidedjourneycoaching.ca
www.facebook.com pjgrouette
www.instagram.com paulinegrouette guidedjourney
www.linkedin.com in pauline grouette 11a8ba216

RISING STRONG:
My Journey from Survival to Success

My name is Jennifer Johnson and I am the owner of True Fashionistas, the largest lifestyle resale store in Florida.

I grew up on a farm in central Minnesota the 2nd oldest of 6 siblings. My dad showed me and my siblings what hard work was like. He worked tirelessly to put food on our table and make ends meet for my family.

My last year in high school I met a boy whom I began dating. He seemed great at first until he started hitting me, and abusing me verbally. I didn't know that the hitting and verbal abuse would be the least of my issues. The physical violence turned into sexual violence with him raping me. It didn't matter that I said no he would continue each and every time. The violence also got worse. It got so bad that when I graduated and was going on to college on a scholarship for broadcast communications (I wanted to be a TV news anchor so bad) he threatened to kill me if I ended up going. I never went to college because I was so scared.

The turning point was one night he drove me off the road and tried to kill me. Something changed in me that night. Something just clicked and I realized this is not how I want to live my life. I feel it was as though God was talking to me saying get out now while you are still alive. It was by that grace of God that I did get out. Over the course of the next few months I was able to distance myself from him, get a restraining order and take my life back. This was something I really did on my own because I didn't want anyone to think less of me or not believe me. It was a very tough time but I drew on my faith (even though I didn't understand it at the time) to get me through.

This entire experience changed me. At the time I thought it was terrible, and it was, but now 30+ years later reflecting on this entire experience I learned so much about myself and about resilience. Your past becomes part of the fabric that you are today. You use your past to change you future and to make your future even better.

I realize that no matter what you are facing there will be light at the end of the tunnel and things in life happen FOR you not TO you! The reason all of this happened to me was so that now, later in life, I am able to go out and speak to people and motivate them and I do just that. From small stages to large stages to intimate events. I speak about what happened to me, how I got out and what I am doing with what happened to me now. f I can help just ONE person then what I went through was all worth it.

I harnessed all that negativity, violence and pain and went on to become Ms. Petite MN, a model and actress and advocate for stopping sexual violence.

I am now an entrepreneur (I owe 3 different companies) as well as an author, small business coach and professional speaker. I use all that life has thrown at me and use it to encourage others.

My goal is to continue speaking in front of audiences world wide to spread the voice of encouragement, resilience and hope.

I invite each of you to look at your own life and the challenges that you have faced along the way. What have they taught you? What were the lessons, as there always lessons in everything that happens for us. It is our job to find out what those lessons are, learn from them and teach them to others so it can better their lives.

I didn't allow the challenges of my past to hold me down. I took the challenges of my past and harnessed them to create a better future for myself I used them to propel me to become UNSTOPPABLE!

Jennifer Ann Johnson

From national model to founder of a successful resale empire, Jennifer Johnson embodies entrepreneurial grit and grace. As the visionary behind True Fashionistas, Florida's largest lifestyle resale store, she's mastered building a thriving business while maintaining personal well-being. Her Amazon bestseller and award-winning podcast offer a blueprint for success that resonates with business owners everywhere.

Jennifer's impact extends far beyond her own achievements. As a coach and speaker, she's transformed countless entrepreneurs' lives through her online academy and coaching programs. Her expertise, featured in Forbes and Vogue, coupled with her dynamic presence from national TV appearances, captivates and inspires action.

Recognized as a Gulfshore Life Businesswoman of the Year, Jennifer doesn't just teach success – she embodies it. Her blend of experience, strategies, and motivational energy empowers audiences to achieve their dreams.

Facebook: www.facebook.com/profile.php?id=100089312054101&mibextid=LQQJ4d
Instagram: Jennifer.ann_johnson
Linkedin: www.linkedin.com/in/jennifer-johnson-39237448/
True FashionistasFacebook: www.facebook.com/truefashionistasresale/
Instagram: truefashionistasresale

EMPOWERHER CONTENT DAY

at

Elevate Your Brand Through Creative And Impactful Content!

EmpowerHer Content Day equips attendees with the tools and knowledge needed to craft compelling content for social media, podcasts, and videos.

FEBRUARY 22, 2025

TOTAL ACCESS TICKET: $127

WWW.SHERISESSTUDIOS.COM

by Ashleigh Netter

BETTING ON YOURSELF: NAVIGATING LIFE'S STORMS FOR AUTHENTIC SUCCESS

Imagine having everything in place: a stable job, a supportive family, and a bright future. Now imagine losing all of that within 24 hours. How would you feel? Devastated? Confused? Angry? Afraid?

I've felt all of these emotions, but most of all, I've felt numb. Life's storms—whether personal, professional, or environmental—can dismantle everything we've worked for in an instant.

For me, it was on August 29, 2005, when Hurricane Katrina hit New Orleans, Louisiana, with unprecedented force. I went from an aspiring pharmacist student to a survivor navigating the chaos the storm left behind.

The Turning Point

Life's unpredictability shook me to my core, leaving me feeling like I was navigating a storm without a compass. The idea of betting on myself seemed like a gamble, but in this moment it was the most empowering choice I could make. Instead of succumbing to the chaos, I chose to take risks, embrace challenges, and transform my life and career. This encounter sparked the creation of my life's mission: Living to Inspire and Transform (LIT).

Risk #1: *GET L.I.T.! I must live to inspire and transform in everything I do.*

Embracing Life's Storms

Life's storms bring challenges, but instead of avoiding them, embrace them. Each storm teaches us resilience, determination, big-picture thinking, and emotional intelligence. These qualities become our assets —our capital gains. Embrace your storms, own them, and leverage the lessons they provide.

Principle 1: Embrace the Challenge

Every storm, whether a personal setback, a career obstacle, or a financial crisis, comes with its own set of challenges. Embrace these challenges rather than avoid them. They teach us resilience, determination, and the ability to see the bigger picture. These qualities become your capital gains—valuable assets that you can leverage for authentic success.

Principle 2: Inspire Through Your Journey

Authentic success isn't just about personal achievement; it's about inspiring others. Listen and reflect before responding. This practice allows you to check your emotional capacity and respond effectively. When you find yourself in others' stories and build genuine connections, you not only inspire hope but also create a supportive network.

Principle 3: Transform with Gratitude

Practice daily gratitude, especially for the storms. Gratitude transforms every area of life, fostering an environment of kindness, respect, and support. This mindset benefits you and those around you, creating a community of growth and support.

Betting on Yourself

Betting on oneself means taking risks and embracing the unknown with confidence. It's about believing in your ability to overcome obstacles and turn challenges into opportunities.

Here's how you can do it:

- **Acknowledge Your Strengths:** Recognize and celebrate your abilities and achievements. This boosts your confidence and prepares you to face new challenges.
- **Set Clear Goals:** Define what success means to you. Set realistic and achievable goals that align with your values and aspirations.
- **Take Calculated Risks:** Step out of your comfort zone and take risks that can lead to growth. Assess the potential outcomes and make informed decisions.
- **Learn from Failures:** View failures as learning opportunities. Analyze what went wrong, learn from it, and apply those lessons to future endeavors.
- **Seek Support:** Surround yourself with supportive individuals who believe in your vision. Their encouragement can provide the motivation needed to keep moving forward.

The Impact of Betting on Yourself

Applying these principles can significantly impact your life and community. Through leadership and influence, you can secure opportunities, create initiatives, and support those in need.

For example, I've been able to secure over $1.5 million in corporate dollars to establish scholarship programs, feed thousands of families, and launch initiatives that provide essential services to underserved communities.

This isn't a flex; it's a testament to what betting on yourself and being L.I.T. can achieve.

My story is a powerful reminder that we all can rise from our personal Katrinas. As you reflect on your life, consider where you can take the risk to bet on yourself. What areas of your life are ripe for change? What dreams have you been putting off because of fear or uncertainty? Now is the time to act. Whether it's starting a new career, launching a business, or pursuing a personal passion, take that leap of faith.

Ask yourself: What do I have to lose? More importantly, what do I have to gain? Success on social media and trending topics often stem from those who dared to bet on themselves. They share their journeys, their failures, and their victories, inspiring others to do the same.

So, share your story. Document your journey. Let your experience inspire others. Use hashtags like #BetOnYourself, #TakeTheRisk, #GetLIT and #AuthenticSuccess to connect with a community of risk-takers and dream-chasers.

My challenge to you is to show up every day betting on yourself. Take risks, embrace your storms, and inspire and transform those around you.

My name is Dr. Ashleigh Netter, and I believe in betting on myself for authentic success. Connect with me on ashleighnetter.com, LinkedIn, Instagram, and YouTube.

by Darlene Taylor

CULTIVATING STRENGTH, SELF-LOVE, AND A PURPOSE-FILLED PATH THROUGH ADVERSITY

Having to endure one life-altering-do-over after another has forged the courage to face whatever comes my way as I know that I have cultivated the strength of character and self-love to weather any storm that may shift its winds my way. Several years ago, I abandoned my career, divorced, and became wholeheartedly focused on my role as a mother. All those life-altering changes sent me on a self-discovery path over the next few years, which morphed into the opportunity of a lifetime to explore and define myself.

MY JOURNEY

I was always a dedicated student to whom academic success was extremely important. I decided to become a therapist at age 14 and never looked back, working hard toward that goal and holding tightly to the idea that a successful career was the most important achievement I could attain. I earned a Master's in Social Work, nurturing a dream to change the world, one family at a time. I focused intently on my career, taking for granted that I would easily fall into the traditional cycle of life - find a husband and have a family.

Naively, I created a plan in my head during graduate school that laid out precisely how adulthood would unfold, but by graduation, I felt behind schedule and pressured to make my current relationship official - despite signs it wasn't the right fit. Determined to cram my life into the box I built, I got married at 28 to someone whose career became the center of our lives and forced me and my career into the back seat.

As a coach's wife, my main priority was to support his career. I still held fast to my career dreams, but whenever I began to gain traction, we had to relocate. Multiple moves meant that I couldn't secure licensure to work as a therapist in each different state, so I eventually switched to teaching and became a professor at The University of Cincinnati. With every move, I began losing myself and focusing more on being the "coach's wife" while my dreams drifted out of focus. Once our daughter was born, my focus turned to being a great mother and I soon lost myself in that role, too.

MY TURNING POINT

Then the biggest "do-over" of all happened - divorce. I had to figure out who I was now and what I wanted the rest of my life to look like. It was clear that going back to my previous career and ideas of success no longer made sense. Life had changed me and I accepted that it was okay to reinvent myself based on my ever-changing circumstances. I now had a responsibility to think about the kind of woman I wanted to model for my daughter and to find the courage to make choices that were authentic to the best version of me. My decision to get a divorce meant giving up everything that I thought embodied success and finding a different path while finding the confidence to believe in myself again. It meant that I had to resurrect my career and decide what being a successful woman and mother would look like. I could let go of everyone else's opinions and finally decide and define what I wanted for myself.

LESSONS LEARNED

Some of the most valuable lessons I learned were:
> It's never too late to start over
> Be fearless
> Let go of the need for the validation of others

The most important thing I did was repair my relationship with the idea of being selfish. I had to embrace that the only way to be successful was to ensure that I was doing the best job of nurturing myself by understanding the true meaning of self-care. I immediately started therapy and medication to deal with the depression that had hampered my ability to

my confidence and get back into the work world. Caring for myself became my priority. I took control of my health focusing on diet, exercise, rest, and overall mental health. I became intentional about learning to listen and trust myself. Meditation and mindfulness were a huge part of my healing process.

We change when the pain of where we are becomes greater than the fear of what comes next. All of the obstacles I faced showed me that though change is scary, it doesn't have to be painful. You get to decide how you enter new experiences because anxiety and excitement are two sides of the same coin, both born from uncertainty, but your mindset determines how you approach the unknown. The best thing you can do is flow with change because it is the one certainty in life.

Surround yourself with people who empower you with accountability. Never stop making yourself the priority or let your dreams take a back seat. Know that the right partner will make room in the front seat for both of your dreams. Hold yourself accountable, always giving yourself grace and space to grow.

ACHIEVING SUCCESS

I see success through the lives changed by sharing my story and guiding others through my book and coaching program. I have used every obstacle as a springboard to the next phase of my career and accomplished things I never thought I would by starting businesses and achieving my childhood dream of writing a book. Most importantly, I learned to measure my success by the lives I touch, not by the money I make or outward accolades.

I plan to continue coaching women helping them uncover their uniqueness and leverage those strengths to achieve the life of their dreams. I will continue teaching the importance of wellness and balance, permitting women to define success for themselves.

REFLECTION AND ACTION

I challenge others to re-introduce yourself to YOU. Become intimately familiar with your gifts and begin using them more intentionally and fruitfully. Compare your life with the vision you dare to dream, and then make concrete goals to be accountable to yourself to make that vision your reality.

www.darlenetaylor.com
www.darlenetaylor.com/social-links
darlene@darlenetaylor.com

FENIX TV: THE MAGIC BEHIND OUR LUXURY GIFTING SUITE FOR EMMYS WEEK

by Hanna Olivas

As the Chief Branding Officer of FENIX TV, I'm thrilled to share a glimpse of what we're preparing for this year's Emmy's Week. There's a certain buzz in the air as the industry's most talented creators, storytellers, and visionaries gear up for one of the most exciting events in television: the Emmys. This year, we're elevating the celebration with our luxury gifting suite, where art, creativity, and the beauty of collaboration come together in one exclusive space.

Imagine walking the red carpet, surrounded by the energy and glamour of Hollywood's brightest stars. Our gifting suite is where the industry's top talent will gather—not just for the luxurious gifts, but to connect, celebrate, and reflect on what it takes to create television that moves, entertains, and challenges audiences. It's a rare opportunity for those who live and breathe creativity to come together and recognize the incredible artistry behind the scenes.

What I find truly inspiring about this event is that it's not just about the glitz and glamour. Yes, there will be stunning red carpet moments, but our focus is on celebrating the magic behind the camera—the untold stories of the creative process. There's something profoundly fascinating about understanding what it takes to bring a show or film to life. Most people see the finished product, but the real magic happens in the countless hours of writing, designing, editing, and collaborating to create something exceptional.

At FENIX TV, we want to shine a spotlight on the unsung heroes—the screenwriters who pour their hearts into scripts, the directors who bring stories to life, the set designers who transform ideas into immersive worlds, and the sound engineers who make every note resonate. The Emmy nominees we honor this year represent the best of this craft. They're not just talented individuals; they're visionaries who have pushed the boundaries of what television can be. Their work challenges conventions, tells bold stories, and leaves an indelible mark on the industry.

One of the things I'm most excited about is offering a behind-the-scenes look at what really goes into making a show or film. We're opening a window into the creative process, revealing the dedication, collaboration, and artistry that many people never get to see. The Television Academy and the Emmys are more than just a night of awards—they're a celebration of the countless hours of work, the late nights, the breakthroughs, and the passion that drive this industry.

Our luxury gifting suite is designed to be a place where art, luxury, and inspiration converge. We've curated a collection of premium gifts from brands that align with our vision of creativity and excellence. But more than that, we want this space to be one where those who've dedicated their lives to storytelling can take a moment to reflect, recharge, and connect with like-minded creators.

As I look forward to this event, I can't help but feel a deep sense of excitement and pride. The Emmy's Week gifting suite is more than just an event; it's a celebration of the craft that I hold close to my heart. It's about honoring the brilliance that happens behind the scenes, the unsung work that leads to those shining moments on stage.

This year's Emmys aren't just a recognition of talent; they're a tribute to the power of storytelling, the creativity that drives our industry, and the extraordinary individuals who make it all possible. We can't wait to celebrate with you and share this incredible experience. After all, it's moments like these that remind us why we fell in love with television and film in the first place—because of the stories that move us, the art that inspires us, and the people who make it all come alive.

LIFESTYLE &
Wellness

by Christina Collura

AUTISM ADVOCACY TO ENTREPRENEURIAL SUCCESS

"If they can't learn the way we teach – maybe we should teach they way we learn".

A quote that I always lived by and it became even more apparent after my son's Autism diagnosis. My name is Christina Collura, I am a mom of two boys, a full-time educator, turned Autism advocate and an award-winning entrepreneur. I was married for almost 12 years and in that time, faced the most challenging realization – my youngest son is Autistic. At that time, I was also dealing with Stage 4 endometriosis which required extensive surgery to even be able to tackle the ups and downs of my son's diagnosis and of course, my own life, insecurities and anxiety.

With Luca (my son's) diagnosis came the "AH-HA" moment, and a turning point that went back to the very quote that you read at the beginning. Luca's diagnosis wasn't going to be a barrier, but simply a leaning curve for everyone that he encountered- figuring out how he needed to learn. This completely changed my mentality both professional and personally and made the quote even more blinding!

Luca loved the texture and using chalk as a catalyst for coloring, scribbling etc.He could spend all day scribbling and doodling on my driveway. I decided to put that interest to good use and apply it to a wooden name puzzle. I hand painted a chalkboard base to the indented spaces of the puzzle – and watched his fine motor skills develop – with not being able to go "out of the lines" as he wrote the letters in his name L-u-c-a. 4 weeks later – this spiraled onto paper and my mind was blown! How did I just come up with an idea to help my son to learn to successfully write his name?

I took this idea – literally googled a manufacturer overseas (who turned out to be one of the biggest in China), got a prototype made for and Uppercase and Numbers 1-20 puzzle (with a chalkboard base) and brought the successful concept into my Kindergarten classroom and saw the same success!! The difference was – many other children – both on and off the spectrum – wanted to play!! An inclusive product concept that just brought children of all needs and abilities together! Did I just do this? Facing my own obstacles, demons, fears, I took the idea and ran with it. We are currently a fast-growing brand with a patented concept that is reaching more and more children, while advocating and spreading inclusivity along the way.

Throughout this process, I continue to look back and realize that I am the only one that could have made this happen. People often ask me "how did I get here?".My response is always "one day at a time". That stands true with battling the challenges of Autism everyday! I continue to learn and grow with my son – one day at a time.

Being named Top 100 Inspirational Woman through my work with Autism Awareness, An RBC Woman of Influence Nominee, Mom's Choice Award Winner, Parent's Pick Award Winner, Total Mom Pitch Top 100 (to name a few) – I continue to have pinch me moments – but the reality is – it all comes back to the one decision I made after my son's diagnosis – to figure out how he needed to learn! That was the most important decision I made with that tough diagnosis.

I inspire all woman out there to make the best possible decision for both you and your family. Forget about what everyone else is going to think – and decide your own path and go for it! You'll never be disappointed for trying – you'll be more disappointed for not!

Becoming a successful entrepreneur while raising an autistic child requires resilience, adaptability, and a unique set of skills. Here are some key ideas that I continue to draw upon from such a journey

RESILIENCE AND PERSEVERANCE

- **Never Give Up:** The journey is filled with challenges, from balancing parenting responsibilities with business demands to overcoming societal stigma. Resilience is key.

- **Embrace Failures:** Viewing setbacks as learning opportunities rather than failures can propel growth and improvement.

TIME MANAGEMENT AND PRIORITIZATION

- **Effective Time Management:** Balancing business and personal responsibilities requires meticulous planning and prioritization.
- **Delegation:** Learning to delegate tasks in business and seeking support in parenting (e.g., from family, friends, or professional caregivers) is crucial.

ADAPTABILITY AND FLEXIBILITY

- **Stay Adaptable:** Both business and parenting can be unpredictable. Being flexible and adaptable helps in navigating sudden changes and challenges.
- **Creative Problem-Solving:** Finding creative solutions for both business hurdles and parenting challenges can make a significant difference.

ADVOCACY AND AWARENESS

- **Raise Awareness:** Being an advocate for autism awareness can create a supportive community and potentially open business opportunities.
- **Network and Connect:** Building a strong network of other parents, professionals, and business connections can provide emotional support and practical advice.

SELF-CARE AND MENTAL HEALTH

- **Prioritize Self-Care:** Taking care of oneself is crucial to avoid burnout. This includes finding time for rest, hobbies, and mental health care.
- **Seek Professional Help:** Therapy or counseling can provide support for managing stress and maintaining mental well-being.

FINANCIAL MANAGEMENT

- **Smart Financial Planning:** Careful financial planning and budgeting are essential to manage both business expenses and the costs associated with raising a child with special needs.
- **Seek Funding and Grants:** Exploring available funding, grants, or financial aid for both business and autism-related needs can provide additional support.

EDUCATION AND LEARNING

- **Continuous Learning:** Keeping up with both business trends and the latest in autism research and therapies can provide valuable insights and strategies.
- **Leverage Resources:** Utilizing available resources such as online courses, support groups, and business mentorship programs can aid in personal and professional growth.

EMPATHY AND COMPASSION

- **Empathetic Leadership:** Leading with empathy and understanding can create a positive work environment and build strong relationships with clients and employees.
- **Teaching Inclusivity:** Promoting inclusivity and understanding within the business can set a positive example and create a supportive community.

CELEBRATING SMALL WINS

- **Celebrate Milestones:** Recognizing and celebrating small victories, both in business and personal life, can boost morale and provide motivation to keep going.
- **Practice Gratitude:** Maintaining a positive outlook and practicing gratitude can improve overall well-being and provide a sense of accomplishment.

You really are your own worst critique; but I also know I have one (two) sweet boys that need my drive and dedication! I need it too! You can and will do it – you just need to put your mind to it to become the most "unstoppable" version of yourself!

Christina Collura
Full Time Educator of 20 years
CEO AND FOUNDER – Creative Beginning

WOMEN ON THE
Rise

by Alina Timofeeva

FROM CLEANING TOILETS TO GLOBAL STAGES: THE EDUCATIONAL JOURNEY OF ALINA TIMOFEEVA

Alina Timofeeva's journey is a powerful testament to resilience and the transformative power of education. Born in a small village in post-Soviet Russia, her path from washing toilets at McDonald's in Russia to becoming a prominent figure in technology in London, UK, underscores her unwavering determination and passion for learning. This article explores Alina's educational journey, highlighting how her relentless pursuit of knowledge paved the way for her success.

EARLY BEGINNINGS AND SELF-EDUCATION

Growing up in a poor family, Alina was raised with the expectation that her future would be confined to traditional gender roles. However, she felt destined for more. Alina's thirst for knowledge became evident early on. At just eight years old, she taught herself English using old audiotapes—a skill that would become invaluable. Her academic potential was recognized when she won the prestigious Moscow State University Olympiad at 14, granting her direct admission to a specialized mathematics school. This achievement marked the beginning of a series of academic successes.

Continuing her trajectory of excellence, Alina secured another Olympiad win at 16, earning a full scholarship to Moscow State University (MSU). At MSU, she pursued both a Bachelor's and a Master's degree in Mathematics, honing her analytical and problem-solving skills in a rigorous academic environment.

EXPANDING HORIZONS AT THE LONDON SCHOOL OF ECONOMICS

Alina's academic journey extended beyond Russia. Determined to broaden her horizons, she pursued a second Master's degree in Risk and Finance at the prestigious London School of Economics (LSE). This transition came with its challenges, as she navigated the competitive UK job market, often feeling out of place among peers from more privileged backgrounds. Nevertheless, her solid academic foundation and determination saw her through these obstacles.

OVERCOMING BARRIERS

Despite her impressive educational background, Alina faced significant challenges in her early career. Navigating societal expectations and professional etiquette in the UK proved challenging. Her tenacity was tested as she applied for 500 jobs and faced 497 rejections before securing a graduate analyst position at Accenture. This experience highlighted her resilience—a hallmark of her journey.

Alina faced further challenges in her career, particularly during her first promotion attempt. With the guidance of a senior mentor, she rediscovered her confidence and self-worth, leading to a successful promotion just a year after being deemed as failing. Her perseverance paid off, as she was promoted four times in four years—an impressive feat in the male-dominated tech industry.

TENACITY SHAPING CAREER JOURNEY

Today, in her early thirties, Alina is a multi-award-winning strategic advisor in Data & Technology, serving the C-suite of major financial services organizations. She holds a board position at The Chartered Institute for IT and is a thought leader, sought-after speaker, and role model in the tech industry. Her work with leading consulting firms like Oliver Wyman, KPMG, and Accenture has earned her numerous accolades, including Digital Leader of the Year, Digital Transformation Leader, Cloud Professional of the Year, and Most Inspirational Individual of the Year.

SPEAKING ON GLOBAL STAGES

Alina has become a prominent voice on Data and Technology, speaking at high-profile events like the World Economic Forum, London Tech Week, and Money 20/20. She has also shared her insights at prestigious institutions, including the University of Oxford and the London School of Economics. Her TEDx talk, "Fail but Never Give Up," has garnered over 510,000 views, translated into 23 languages, and ranks among the top 10 most-watched TEDx talks released in December 2021. In it, she illustrates how failing an exam for a fast-food chain can lead to three university degrees, career success, and becoming a role model for women in technology.

LIFELONG LEARNING AND MENTORSHIP

Throughout her career, Alina has emphasized the importance of lifelong learning and mentorship. Her journey has taught her the significance of acquiring not just knowledge but also the ability to navigate unspoken societal codes. By seeking mentorship and continually learning, she has overcome biases and thrived in traditionally male-dominated fields.

GIVING BACK

Alina's commitment to education extends beyond her achievements. She founded Unique. Bold. You, an initiative supporting individuals from diverse backgrounds to persevere despite failures. She actively coaches others, particularly women in technology and those from underprivileged backgrounds, guiding them through their educational and professional journeys. As a TEDx speaker and LinkedIn Top Voice in Technology, she aims to inspire 50 million people globally to view failure as an opportunity for growth, whether in technology or personal endeavors.

Alina Timofeeva's educational journey serves as a powerful reminder of the transformative potential of education. From teaching herself English to excelling at two of the world's most prestigious universities, her story is one of relentless pursuit of knowledge. Alina's journey demonstrates that with determination, resilience, and a commitment to learning, one can overcome even the most daunting challenges.

Breaking Barriers: Transforming Adversity into Leadership as an Immigrant Woman

by Tamanna Ramesh

A decade ago, a determined young woman from a small town in India arrived in the United States, fueled by dreams of a better future. Despite the promise of new opportunities, her journey was fraught with challenges—cultural adjustments, language barriers, workplace toxicity, and the complexities of the U.S. immigration system. Yet, her unwavering commitment to personal and professional growth powered her through these obstacles.

From the outset, integrating into the American workplace proved difficult due to cultural differences and the complex immigration system. The Green Card process was particularly daunting, with the EB2 category's wait time exceeding 130 years—a formidable barrier. Professionally, she faced pay equity issues and the constant need to prove herself, especially as a woman in STEM. These obstacles were compounded by harassment, discrimination, and the everyday stress of navigating a new country. Nevertheless, she transformed these adversities into opportunities for growth.

Her journey was marked by an impressive achievement: securing $135,000 in scholarships and assistantships, which funded her STEM graduate degree and part-time MBA program in the U.S. This financial support was crucial, allowing her to focus on her education without incurring significant debt. Over the years, she honed her networking strategies and perfected her negotiation tactics, landing dream jobs at Fortune 500 companies and making five unconventional career pivots. Each move was a calculated step towards building her personal brand and significantly increasing her compensation.

A defining moment in her life came when she secured her Green Card at the age of 29, breaking through the historic wait time barrier by qualifying under the EB1 category—one of the most challenging categories for Indian nationals. This achievement was not just a personal victory but a profound symbol of new beginnings. Free from immigration uncertainty, she could finally pursue her aspirations fully.

With renewed determination, she committed to continuous personal and professional development, advancing from a researcher to a director at a Fortune 100 company. This remarkable progression was driven by hard work, perseverance, and the invaluable support of mentors and sponsors who nurtured her potential. She also took on leadership roles in professional organizations, notably with the Institute of Food Technologists, where she served as Chair of the Product Development Division and the Women's Resource Group. These roles amplified her influence and established her as a thought leader in the food and beverage industry.

Throughout her journey, she faced numerous unseen challenges: over performing while underpaid, dealing with bad managers, experiencing burnout and imposter syndrome, and confronting biases and systemic barriers. While the highs on her LinkedIn profile are visible, the lows—marked by harassment, bullying, and the grueling immigration process—were equally significant. Despite these struggles, she chose to fight, paving her own path with resilience and determination.

Her experiences taught her that success is not solely defined by titles or financial gain but by the freedom and empowerment to pursue one's own path. Perseverance, adaptability, and continuous learning were essential to overcoming adversity and achieving success.

To those navigating similar challenges, she advises remaining resilient and proactive. Seek out mentors and sponsors for guidance and support, and invest in continuous learning to enhance your skills and adaptability. Challenges often present opportunities for significant personal growth and success.

Today, she stands as a leader at a Fortune 100 company and the founder of Spark Career Services, dedicated to supporting underrepresented individuals in their career journeys. Through Spark Career Services, she helps others overcome barriers, achieve career advancement, and drive equity in the workplace. Her goal is to empower one million individuals to break through barriers and achieve career fulfillment, with a commitment to fostering workplace wellness and championing purpose-driven careers.

Call to Action for All the Amazing Women Out There:

- **ASK** for those high-visibility projects, raises, and promotions that you deserve.
- **BALANCE** by prioritizing your well-being to avoid burnout and undue stress.
- **CHALLENGE** biases and systemic barriers that stand in your way.

Contact:
www.sparkcareerservices.com
www.linkedin.com/company/spark-career-services
www.linkedin.com/in/tamannaramesh
www.instagram.com/spark_your_career

sparkcareerservicesllc@gmail.com

by Angelica Kapsis

PIONEERING VETERAN TRANSFORMING U.S. ELECTIONS

Angelica Kapsis, President of VotRite

Angelica Kapsis is the President and Co-Founder of VotRite, a South Florida company dedicated to re-shaping how elections are conducted in the United States. With Angelica at the helm, VotRite is determined to make the future of local, state, and national elections more accessible, more secure, and more transparent for all. VotRite is also committed to maintaining an environment free from bullying and harassment. Angelica ensures her team is treated with dignity while being held to above higher than average standards for their performance.

Angelica is a dedicated professional with a diverse background in forensic science, psychology, and human services. She holds a Masters in Science in Forensic Science from National University as well as a Bachelor of Science in Psychology from Stony Brook University, showcasing her strong commitment to education and continuous learning.

In addition to her incredible academic career, Angelica is an accomplished Navy Veteran. She has built her life and career on fighting for those in need. As the President and Co-Founder of VotRite, Angelica has been instrumental in developing strategies to enhance voting software accessibility, particularly focusing on ADA (Americans with Disabilities Act) compliance and preferences for individuals with disabilities.

Angelica is also the Founder at Scorpion Fitness Centers, a position that reflects her passion for promoting health and wellness. She has crafted unique fitness plans for members and leads classes, including those catered to individuals with disabilities, in order to guarantee success for clients.

Beyond her professional endeavors, Angelica's dedication to community service is evident through her involvement in various volunteer activities. Angelica has worked as a firefighter, a mentor, and has advocated for at-risk populations. She is also a NASM Certified Personal Trainer and holds CPR & First Aid Certification. Angelica's multifaceted skill set, coupled with her unwavering dedication to social causes, positions her as a versatile and compassionate professional dedicated to making a truly positive impact in her community and beyond.

Angelica is a passionate advocate for technological innovation and creativity. Her company, VotRite, stands at the forefront of electoral innovation, offering cutting-edge voting solutions designed to revolutionize the democratic process. Committed to inclusivity and integrity, VotRite ensures that every voter, regardless of ability or background, can participate in hack-proof elections with confidence. With a steadfast dedication to neutrality and transparency, VotRite's unbiased approach guarantees that election results are trustworthy and immune to contestation. By prioritizing ADA compliance, customizable features, and a commitment to impartiality, VotRite is leading the charge towards fair and equitable elections, where every voice is heard and every vote counts.

To work beside her in achieving her mission, Angelica has selected only those that share her passionate dream and have the knowledge to follow through. Jim Kapsis, VotRite's CEO, has extensive management and technology capabilities and has been the leader of various voting companies in the last 30 years. He has created two patents for voting integration and copyright software. Christopher H. Baum, the company's Chief Compliance Officer, has spent more than 30 years delivering high-quality IT analysis and services on the use of technology in government and in the election industry in particular. Baum currently manages certification processes and ensures election integrity.

As of 2024, VotRite has been officially nominated for this year's Technology Innovator Awards hosted by Innovation in Business, as well as nominated for the 2024 Education and Training Awards hosted by Corporate Vision. It is because of Angelica's unwavering dedication and determination that her company has achieved success, and she has persevered in spite of pushback from other Electronic Voting Machine organizations. Angelica has offered her knowledge and expertise to a variety of media outlets, including the podcast Everyday's Saturday - USMC Veteran and Authority Magazine. She will also be featured in upcoming episodes of the HomeFront Sitrep Podcast as well as the Implementors Podcast.

The SHE RISES STUDIOS PODCAST

The She Rises Studios podcast is dedicated to empowering women like you to reach their full potential and live their best lives. With inspiring stories, insightful interviews, and practical advice from experts in different industries, our podcast is your go-to source for information, inspiration, and motivation. Join us as we explore topics like:

- Overcoming self-doubt and limiting beliefs
- Building and running a successful business
- Building confidence and Self-esteem
- Navigating career transitions
- Starting and growing a business
- Balancing work and family life
- Improving physical and mental health
- Finding meaning and purpose in life
- So many more

Our guests include successful entrepreneurs, inspiring thought leaders, and everyday women who have overcome challenges and achieved their dreams. Each episode is packed with actionable tips and strategies to help you take your life to the next level.

ELIZABETH REECE

Who I Help?

Those who seek to break a habit, leave an abusive relationship, resign from a company where ethics and values are compromised daily and find that while it might be better, it still feels similar.

How I Do It?

Personalized Interventions, Coaching calls, sometimes daily communication, it is the work between the sessions that creates the most growth and autonomy.

What's in It for You?

The goal for my clients is self-sufficiency. Six to nine months is enough for them to take what they need and apply the learning daily in their lives. I always remain available as a friend. I offer a safe space for you to explore anything at any time.

SERVICES:

Coaching, Online Workshops, Retreats in the South of France (Partners for Wellbeing & Coaching Retreats *www.domaine-desmontarels.com*)

We build your program together according to your overarching goal. Re-contracting at anytime, should your requirements change.

GET CONNECTED

- www.quietwaters.space
- www.instagram.com/seeking_quietwaters
- www.facebook.com/elizabethreece.coaching
- www.linkedin.com/in/elizabeth-reece-msc-appcp-26357a14

Made in the USA
Monee, IL
07 July 2026

56546299R00024